SUMMARY: GEOFFREY MOORE'S CROSSING THE CHASM

45 MINUTES - KEY POINTS
SUMMARY / REFRESHER WITH CRIB SHEET
INFOGRAPHIC

EXECUTIVE READS

CONTENTS

Welcome to this Executive Reads summary of Crossing the Chasm by Geoffrey Moore. A production of Kronos Books, produced by the Executive Reads editorial team, edited by Richard Finn.

This summary is meant to provide insight into the Crossing the Chasm book if you are considering reading it or providing you with a refresher of the concepts contained therein if you already read it.

Executive Reads (2015-08-15). Crossing the Chasm: Marketing and Selling Disruptive Products to Mainstream Customers by Geoffrey A. Moor | Book summary. Executive Reads. Paperback Edition.

ISBN: 9798637921294

INTRODUCTION

Underlying the strategy of technology entrepreneurs and the ideas taught in countless business courses lies the book, *Crossing the Chasm: Marketing and Selling High-Tech Products to Mainstream Customers*, by acclaimed author Geoffrey A. Moore. Most new gadgets, software offerings, and hot new web sites initially look promising or experience rapid growth, but often quite can't manage to get the expected success over the long-term. Despite this the technology sector saw the rise of many startups to become multimillion dollar companies - luring other entrepreneurs every day to try their luck. It's seen as a legitimate way to get rich quick. Yet, few succeed. This product management and marketing guide lit the path of many a new offering in the rough and tumble technology markets – both consumer and enterprise.

One might say about almost any failed product that it wasn't bad but somehow couldn't manage to achieve the expected response from the market. It might get a promising burst of growth in the beginning, but then the craze fades and the company faces a situation where they don't know what to do. Almost every time the blame comes down to the marketing of the product. The book *Crossing the Chasm* acts as a guide for any new tech product launched into an uncertain market. It explains how to manage the product marketing launch and how to keep the initial success rolling.

In showing how to follow initial success the book describes that the greatest challenge for any high technology product comes down to the transition from the early market, having just a few visionaries and early adopters, to the large mainstream market, which is dominated by pragmatists. This often ignored gap looms so large that it has been described as a *chasm*. The products that manage to cross this chasm survive and the ones which can't simply perish. The book explains why it's so important to focus on the chasm and why it's so urgent to cross this for any high technology product. It includes a roadmap to make this transition from the early market stage to the large mainstream markets.

Crossing the Chasm features prominently on the shelf of "must reads" for everyone who is a stakeholder of a technological venture.

Executive Reads Rating

IMPORTANT CONCEPTS

Technology Adoption Life Cycle: The product adoption curve for high-tech products representing the relative number of buyers through time. From left (earliest) to right (later) customer categories: Innovators, Early Adopters, Early Majority, Late Majority, Laggards. In other contexts this is called the *Product Adoption Curve.*

The Chasm: The gap between Early Adopters and the Early Majority which so many high-tech products find impossible to cross.

Technology Enthusiasts: High-tech consumers who "geek out" on new products for their own sake. (Innovators)

Visionaries: High-tech product buyers who see where new products are headed and like to be at the forefront in order to match them with strategic opportunity. (Early Adopters)

Pragmatists: Low-profile technology consumers who make prudent, low-risk, buying decisions but still look to new products used by their peers and shown to be useful. (Early Majority/Late Majority)

Conservatives: In the context of high-tech product buyers, these consumers like mature products bundled into discounted packages, including ancillary services. (Late Majority/Laggards)

Continuous Innovation: A new product offering which does not require a change in behavior.

Discontinuous Innovation: A new product offering requiring users to change how they perform relevant actions or what equipment they require to solve their problem.

High-Tech Marketing Model: Marketing a product to the categories of the Technology Adoption Life Cycle in order.

Whole Product: The product, ancillary products, and services around them (an ecosystem or marketplace) comprise all that is needed by the consumer to solve their larger problem.

Target-Customer Characterization: Developing customer images (or personas) which represent the individual buyers and users of a new product within the given market segment.

THE TECHNOLOGY ADOPTION LIFE CYCLE

Consider the quieter, economical and environment friendly electric car. When do you plan to buy such a product? Your answer to that question reveals where you fall along the Technology Adoption Life Cycle curve?

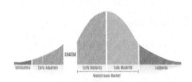

IF YOU BOUGHT a kit and already made an electric car, then you're an *innovator*. If you want to be among the first people in your neighborhood to purchase an electric car then you are an *early adopter*. If you want to buy the electric car when the car has proven its worth, you think you can afford to put your money, and you it as you have seen it doing well with other early adopter owners then you are among *early majority*. If you still don't adopt at this stage and keep waiting until most of the people around you have already switched to the electric car then you are part of the *late majority*. And, if you completely refuse to give up your previous gas running car for the new and the better electric car then you are a *laggard* according to the technology adoption curve.

These terms become very important in the marketing sense. You've probably heard them before and not realized where they came from. Our attitudes about technology and risk become important every time we get introduced to products that require us to change the way we currently live or to change the associated services we currently use. Products requiring such a change are called *discontinuous innovations* and the others which just require normal upgrading of products with no change in the behavior are called *continuous innovations*.

The frequency of launching *discontinuous innovations* in other industries isn't as high as it is in the technological sector. While the other industries launch products which are continuous innovations, the technological sector keeps introducing *discontinuous innovations* quite frequently and that is why the *Technology Adoption Life Cycle* has become a great tool for the marketing and strategy departments of all the tech companies around the world.

As mentioned, the different groups being described in the *Technology Adoption Life cycle* are:

- *Innovators*
- *Early Adopters*
- *Early majority*
- *Late majority*
- *Laggards*

. . .

THE *INNOVATORS* eagerly try out new products without a second thought. They might even pursue a new product really aggressively, showing their urge to be the first to get hands on to a new technology. They might even try out products when the company hasn't launched with any formal marketing campaign. This stems from their innate interest in technology for its own sake. For *innovators* technology is more important than the product as a whole and they enjoy exploring new technologies. A market only contains a small number of *innovators* but if a product manages to win their hearts then the positive impression created in their mind might translate onto the other groups if the firm understands this group and how to leverage their interest.

The *early adopters* share enthusiasm for technology with innovators, but only so much as it achieves business goals. They're not exactly technology enthusiasts, but see the strategic benefits of new technologies. Change doesn't scare them, nor a little risk on a new technology. If they see a great advantage of some product then they consider its benefits in their buying decision. A new market really starts to become serious with these type of customers because they don't need any references to buy a product and usually make decisions on the basis of their own intuition and vision, yet they buy in service of a true business goal.

The next category, the *early majority,* might embrace new technology but have a high sense of practicality associated with their decision making. They want a product proven for other consumers before they buy it for themselves. This section is one of the largest in the curve and has almost one third of the total population of the adoption life cycle. Long-term success necessitates winning this category.

While the *early majority* is quite comfortable in

embracing the new technology once it has proven its worth, the *late majority* sees (and avoids) more risk with a new technology. The buyers in this category want an established product - or even de facto standard - before they are forced to adopt it. Also quite large, almost one third of the entire market of the *technology adoption life cycle* lies here.

Finally, we come to the *laggards*. The people in this category refuse to adopt any new technology product for varied reasons ranging from personal to economic. They buy a product only when it has become so popular that it's now sold embedded in some other common product. This category isn't worth putting any attention from the marketing perspective.

THE HIGH-TECH MARKETING Model

According to the *High-Tech Marketing Model* the best way to develop a market is to work the curve from left to right. This means that you first focus on the *innovators*, then *early adopters* followed by the *early majority* and the *late majority* which could be carried at last to even the *laggards*. The key here lies in focusing on one category of market first so that success there translates to success further along the curve. Each group acts as a reference base for attacking the next group, where the product establishes beachheads in a particular niche.

Building on the references from a previous category into the next category creates momentum and gives rise to a *bandwagon effect*. If the shift from one category to the next occurs smoothly the momentum is carried forth. Imagine Tarzan swinging from vine to vine. Failure to carry momentum forward is similar to Tarzan failing to catch the next vine when he should and just limply swaying back and forth. In this case the other animals would just wait for him to fall and the same happens with companies. When the company delays too much then they just keep hanging in the middle, going nowhere and the rest of the players in the market just wait to see it fall. Trying to make the leap with too much of a delay or without creating a beachhead leaves no support in the next category. If momentum fades often firms will try to jump-start it with haphazard and desperate promotions. The market interprets herky-jerky moves as the signs of desperation they are and wait for the price to effectively drop to 0 or some other alternative arrives.

In addition to marketing one's own products momentum helps keep ahead of the next emerging technologies, which are potential competitors for the product. In all likelihood the next disruptive technology is chasing your product along the adoption curve. Time is short.

Smooth transitions from one stage to the next stage of the *Technology Adoption Life Cycle,* then, become essential. If a firm achieves success in a major new market segment first then it could enjoy a virtual monopoly and end up owning a highly profitable market for quite a long time.

Lotus 1-2-3 used the first edition of this book to achieve and maintain a hold in their market for quite sometime. Their lack of subsequent new products, however, eventually led to to their decline. The *innovators* liked the spreadsheet program because it was fast and slick, the *early adopters* liked it because of the fact that it had some added advantages which they were not getting in any other spreadsheet programs, such as the *What if analysis*, feature. The *early majority* also liked it because it was in line with some of the business operations that they had to do on a daily basis. And finally when it became so popular and most of the people started using the program it became difficult to use any other thing and thus the *late majority* also joined in.

When a product enters the mainstream market, the next product in the pipeline should already be working along the curve too. Lotus 1-2-3 failed in this regard and eventually lost to competitors who did.

Examining history drove the development of this model and it's a very useful model for achieving success in the technology sector. But in spite of that it's not the only thing that would lead to success, there are other things as well along with it, which need to be taken care of.

What's wrong with the High-Tech Marketing Model?

This flaw in the model forms the crux of the whole book. For, between the categories of the model, lie gaps. These gaps symbolize the psychological detachment that one group has from the other group. Because of this dissociation one group has from the rest of the groups, it has problems in accepting the new product if it's being presented to them in the same way as it was being presented to the group which just preceded them. So a product traverses these gaps carefully in order to avoid missing the transition from one segment to the next segment.

2

HIGH TECH MARKETING
ENLIGHTENMENT

There are three different market phases for any technology product. The first of these, the *Early Market*, contains the *early adopters* and the *innovators*. Here the *early adopters* try to create a market advantage for themselves by using the newly adopted product. They share a

vision with the innovation and relate to it. Investors and purchasers who find their goals aligned with the company's strategic goals fund the early market. After this comes the *No Market*. 'No Market' is actually not a market but it's the *chasm* that exists between the *early majority* and the *late majority*.

The other market, known as the *Mainstream Market*, contains the Early and Late Majorities, and sits in the waiting mode. It earns this status because the members of this phase want to first see what the results of the early adopters bring to them. They prefer a tried and tested product. This market offers huge profit opportunities and if a company really wants to harness this market then they need to do really well in the first two stages, described above.

Crossing the chasm becomes the key to the success in

this mainstream market. Without it the mainstream market for any product remains elusive and out of reach, leaving the product to perish in the chasm.

FIRST PRINCIPLES

The first step in learning the whole process of doing well in these three stages is to get an actionable definition of *marketing*. "Can we find in the concept of marketing a reasonable basis for taking actions that will predictably and positively affect company revenues?"

This is the purpose of the book. The meaning of marketing is to take certain actions, which help in creating, growing, maintaining, and defending markets. The purpose of marketing is to develop and shape something that is real. Marketing doesn't mean something used to create illusions as the common perception holds.

Now the above definition of marketing definitely requires a new definition for *market* as well. A market is:

 • A set of actual or potential customers...
 • For a given set of products or services...
 • Who have a common set of needs or wants...
 • Who reference each other when making a buying decision.

THE LAST PART of this definition, "Who reference each other when making a buying decision," places particular importance on how the categories of the high-tech market relate to other consumers in the market. This means that in any high tech market the members tend to look around them and see what their peers are using whenever they make a buying decision.

. . .

THE 3 MARKET **Phases**
Early Markets

The *early markets* phase precedes the *chasm*. It's comprised of the *innovators* - or the *technology enthusiasts* - and the *early adopters* - or the *visionaries*. The *early markets* are dominated by the *visionaries,* but it's the *enthusiasts* who provide the initial push to the technology products by realizing the benefits and potential of any new product. So any high tech marketing program should begin by focusing on the *enthusiasts* - the people who appreciate the technology for its own sake. They appreciate the architecture of the product and understand the competitive advantage it gives them relative to the incumbent products in the market. Less reliability, lower levels of after sale support, sometimes even higher prices come with the territory to this group. While they love products without these problems their tolerance is higher.

One of the most popular technology *enthusiasts*, Bill Gates, gave some great products to the world - totally transforming the whole personal computer industry. Later, he lost this status, somewhat, as he began to adopt Machiavellian business practices. Marc Andressen, on the other hand, has tried to keep up with his title as a technology enthusiast; though, even he looks more and more corporate as the competition has risen. Entrepreneurs, like these, find it difficult to continue their innate feel for technology.

Geoffrey Moore, himself, worked with a fellow named David Lichtman at Rand Information Systems in the late 1970s and early 80s. Long before PCs found a mainstream market Lichtman created a PC for himself, which even had a voice synthesizer. His house contained of all sorts of cameras, sound equipment and other electronic toys. Whenever any of his colleagues wanted to ask about how some technological equipment worked they knew to approach David Lichtman first.

The technology enthusiasts perform the initial evaluation of any recently launched product. So, as the first target for any kind of initial marketing effort it's important to focus on the issues which actually matter to them. If we compare the requirements that different categories of members in the *Technology Adoption Life Cycle* have from a product then this category is the one with the least number of requirements. They can survive even with a bare minimum, though a firm might still fail to meet their needs.

So what do they actually require?

• They don't want fancy communication regarding the product. They simply want the actual information about the product presented to them in the most truthful manner and without any hype.

• When they face any problem with the product they want support from someone who is technologically knowledgeable.

• They like to get the latest stuff and often are ready to agree to all the strict non-disclosure agreements for getting it. This provides the company with early feedback from users and hopefully an advocate, not just in his or her own company, but elsewhere in the market as well.

• The most challenging expectation may come when the enthusiast wants a steep discount for being a test user. Either make it available cheaper or make sure price isn't their concern anymore through an incredible offering.

. . .

THE OTHER EARLY market segment is comprised of the *early adopters* or the *visionaries*. They try to match the emerging technology to some strategic opportunity for their firm. These people also possess the capability to translate some insight about an emerging technology into eventual buying of the technology by their organization. As buyers they actually control millions of dollars of budget and sometimes also represent venture capitals that can fund such high tech businesses. Generally, early adopters are recent entrants into such ranks and are thus highly motivated to succeed.

Visionaries put a lot of value on time because, according to them, any opportunity has a certain time window and they want to seize that opportunity before it closes. So if a company wants to realize the benefits from these visionaries, who carry high revenue opportunities, then they would have to deal with a fairly demanding customer.

THE DYNAMICS *of Mainstream Markets*

An *early market* requires an entrepreneurial company and breakthrough technology product enabling a new way of doing business, a technology enthusiast who evaluates and appreciates the advantages of the new product over others, and a visionary who sees how the new product portends a significant shift and who stands willing to spend accordingly. When the market unfolds, the startup begins giving early copies of its products to the technology *enthusiasts* so that they feel excited about the product being launched. It then shares with the *visionaries* its own vision of the future to come. *Visionaries* check with the technology *enthusiasts* who have already tested the product to reality-check the vision and its validity. When the *visionaries* believe it enough then they enter into negotiations with the company. At first the amount of money agreed upon might seem huge, but soon reality sets in: it's just tip of the iceberg. This amount enables the technology *enthusiast* to get more tech toys for themselves, and allows the entrepreneurial company to work on product modifications to achieve the desired product. On paper, the visionary owns or licensed a high potential product, though in reality it's still a dream. The startup wants this outcome, but dangers line this path on all sides - standing in the way of a proper start.

But why would an early market not get a proper start? What could be the problems that might occur?

The First Problem

The first problem arises when the company possesses little or no experience in bringing a new product to the market, which leads to selling to the wrong customer or choosing the wrong sales channel. This situation is often made worse by the lack of capital to support the launch. Many times the inexperienced salespeople attempt to sell the product through inappropriate sales channels. They might even end up promoting the product to the wrong class of customers.

What often goes wrong in this scenario is that the company tries to win an existing great market, an ocean full of the red blood spilled in competition. They seek to be the biggest fish in an already big pond full of many other big fish. Before attempting this, a small startup company should set upon a strategy of selecting a very small pond. This again takes us back to our definition of a market that the members take references from each other. They must be aware of each other as a market group. Rather, the startup should try to become the leader with those small sets of consumers within a niche. The market niche should be a self-referencing market segment whose members know each other and each other's vendors.

By focusing on this small market they take the time to develop their own internal expertise without losing focus on their prime aim: to sell their products. And by the time they have completely dominated that small market they will be ready to expand into the other market segments as well. Building on success in one small market segment leads to achieving success in the next market. Chose the angle of attack wisely and the chain reaction spreads fast and wide.

THE SECOND PROBLEM

The other problem scenario occurs when the company sells a product to a *visionary* before it's ready to be delivered. This kind of situation is commonly known as the *vaporware problem*. A product, with many significant issues to be handled, winds up pre-launched and pre-marketed. In doing this, the company might end up securing some pilot projects but then they start seeing problems when the schedules slip and the deadlines are missed. When this occurs the visionaries, to whom they have sold, start feeling annoyed and take away their support from the company. We have already discussed that time is really important for the these consumers. They need quick and time bound responses. When this type of problem occurs the startup faces a lot of wasted time and effort. No pot of positive customer references, needed for future sales, lies at the end of that rainbow. This is actually a disaster situation for a startup company.

The solution is to shut down all its marketing efforts and focus on a select group of pilot projects. The company should focus all its energy and resources on the singular goal of providing the effective delivery to the customer and creating a deliverable, and marketable, product. This ensures getting that positive customer reference.

THE THIRD PROBLEM

Another problem situation occurs when the company actually fails to provide the customer with a concrete return on investment that can be celebrated as a major step forward. The company impressed the *innovators* but fails to provide the *visionaries* with that compelling application that would lead them to put their money into it. In this situation the company would be able to get the initial sales but then find it difficult to build on early sales and achieve real success.

The right solution for this situation involves a thorough re-evaluation of the product because it's a major conceptual flaw that led to this problem. If it's not actually some breakthrough product then it's probably not going to succeed. Room might exist, however, to get some space in the mainstream market as a supplementary product. The company would need to accept it and thus change their expectations from the product and also change the way they are distributing the product.

On the other hand, if the product actually is a break-through product, then the company faces serious issues. They need to figure out to convince the chosen market of this fact. To do do, they need to create a single application of their product that demonstrates the essential aspect of the product no other alternatives deliver on.

The development of an early market can easily derail because of these common problems. There are multiple solutions to get back on track when the product is just on the starting phase, discussed later on.

Mainstream Markets

The mainstream of the high tech market would look similar to the *mainstream market* of any other sector. The *mainstream markets* are dominated by the *early majority*, also known as the *pragmatists,* in the high tech markets. These market members act as leaders to the *late majority*, the *conservatives* of the high tech market. Down the line we find the *laggards,* or the *skeptics,* who completely reject the *pragmatists* as the market leaders.

DYNAMICS of the Mainstream market phase

So far we discussed how *visionaries* drive the development of the *early market* and the *pragmatists* drive the development of the *mainstream market*. Winning these groups is not only important for entry but also ensures a long-term dominance in the market. To maintain this dominance in the market the product must meet the needs of the chosen user base, but doesn't necessary need to be the really high end and top quality. In that situation, if some other breakthrough product from some competitor emerges then respond appropriately.

How a mainstream market can be lost:

• The company diverts its attention from the research and development of the product and starts investing in some other product or market not within their core competency. For example, instead of focusing on their main product Novell diverted their attention. They began concentrating on porting to mainframe and minicomputers, buying software application companies, and started doing R&D in home appliances. This made them lose their market to Microsoft.

• Or the company itself introduces an inferior version of their already established product. When AutoDesk introduced Release 13 of their already successful and dominant product, AutoCAD, they did just this. The new user interface confused users and the software ran much slower. Customers sought alternatives allowing competitors to make their entry into the market and carve a share out of AuotCADs' hide for themselves.

INSTEAD OF FOCUSING on the mainstream market these firms continued focusing on only the early market. They failed to judge what the requirements of the *mainstream market* were and thus lost their *mainstream market* leadership position. The key to smoothly transitioning from the early majority pragmatists to the late majority conservatives is to maintain a strong relationship with the pragmatists while keeping the conservatives happy with added value for the old infrastructure. Often, adding services and concentrating on the whole product achieves this.

CROSSING *the Chasm*

Between each category of the *Technology Adoption Life Cycle* lie spaces representing credibility gaps when seeking to use one group as a reference in the next. While momentum builds from category to category, they do not reference each other. The greatest of these is *the chasm* between *early adopters* and the *early majority*.

Crossing the chasm involves making a smooth transition from the *early markets* to the *mainstream markets*. The strategy here resembles, in some way, the infamous Allied assault of the beaches of Normandy on D-Day. To make it across the chasm requires an aggressive approach. The main aim of the American force on D-Day was to capture Western Europe. In our case the goal is to capture the *mainstream market* and achieve a leadership position, pushing out the competitors who now dominate.

Similar to that fateful day during Word War II, to enter into this *mainstream market* the company needs to assemble a force of allies - comprised of other products and partner companies. The goal is to make the transition from the early market phase, analogous to England, to the target market segment in the mainstream - the beaches of Normandy. The *invasion force* most absolutely focus on the point of attack. If the startup is able to force any competitor out of the targeted niche, then it can secure that beachhead. Only after this can the product move out of the initial niche to take over additional market segments like the Allied forces captured the districts of France in the D-Day analogy.

The strategy seems quite simple from here. The enemy already captured the area and the available opportunities aren't close to the desired market segments. Do not focus on capturing the whole area first. Find one strategic target segment for entry that helps gain a strategic leadership position in the market. This enables the force to capture other territories and then finally achieve the final goal: full control of "Eisenhower's Europe"; full control of the mainstream market.

This bears repeating: focus on one niche market segment. This market segment needs to be carefully selected for ease of entry and strategic advantage for later capturing other market segments. Concentrate on capturing this segment and winning trust of the market members so that the product becomes the leader in this niche. Once accomplished, then the firm can afford to focus on the next market segment. Gradually, the product moves on to the whole market, segment by segment. Thus, gaining a complete dominance over the *mainstream market*, the original goal.

Seems easy and obvious enough. However, most of the companies fail to perform this task. The main reason for this is that, in spite of focusing on a particular niche, the companies adopt a sales driven strategy. This harms the company's efforts when it's in need of making a transition from the *early markets* to the *mainstream markets*. It's highly tempting to go for sales at this time. The successful companies, however, are those who are able to take the long-term view and do not get carried away by the unfocused sales opportunities they perceive at that time. Being sales driven at this juncture may prove fatal for the fledgling product.

When the company focuses on sales at this time they lose the opportunity to do what is actually required of them: to get hold of the target niche first. The advantages of focusing on target niche is that when you have become a leader of a niche then it becomes easy to move on to other segments. This is because, as previously discussed, the pragmatist buyers like to buy from industry leaders. When a company isn't a market leader then, even if they are getting initial sales, the orders die out soon and they won't be able to build on them and thus wouldn't be able to *cross the chasm*.

GOT THE NICHE MARKET- WHAT NOW?

The product now has achieved what it intended to. First it needed to capture a niche market. Then, build on that strategic position and in order to spread to the wider market. There can be situations when the company achieves this stage and manages to capture the leadership position in the niche market but then doesn't know what to do next. This portends a dangerous situation for a company needing to capitalize on previous success and not lose momentum. The company needs to have a long-term target from the start - a consistent vision all the way through. The achievement of the leadership position in the niche market segment shouldn't be seen as a "mission accomplished". Rather, see it as just a step in the ladder to the ultimate goal.

TARGETING THE NICHE – **What's so difficult**

This formula, in such a situation, will help a product *cross the chasm*. Of course, finding and targeting the right niche for the new product is not as easy as it appears. The selection of this niche is one of the trickiest decisions that the marketer makes.

The first step is to divide the whole market into discrete sets. Then, evaluate the different market segments on the basis of how attractive each one of them is in light of the product's relative strengths. Narrow down the number of market segments under your purview and then examine the finalists closely from all perspectives. After this, the finalists are carefully studied for the market size they carry, distribution networks in the market, and the competitors that are present in these market segments. It's important to estimate how well would the territory be defended by the competition present there. This whole process is termed as *developing the market segmentation strategy*.

3

DECISION MAKING

The high-risk, low-data decision

The task of crossing the chasm is quite high risk. It requires the company to compete with at least one alternative already established in the mainstream market for the particular problem solved. Success in this competition can be rewarding while the consequences of a failure fatal to the product - maybe even resulting in the loss of a great amount of equity value for the company. The main problem is that, along with the associated high risk, there isn't much information available for making an informed decision. Hence, a high risk, low data decision.

In such a situation what people generally would do is to rely upon the existing market reports and the sales estimates given for these markets. But the point here is that these are mere assumptions. Since the new product doesn't exist in the market segment, these estimations rely on assumptions, which may not be relevant. Market analysts create these predictions without actually considering the possibility of introduction of *discontinuous innovations* in the market, which is precisely the aim, so take these reports and analysis with a giant grain of salt. The marketer must honestly accept this lack of hard data in deciding where to make an entry. One needs to rely upon informed intuition and maybe leave out the analytical reasoning a bit.

THE ART of intuitive decision-making

If analytical reasoning provides limited value in such a situation, the marketer must rely upon the art of *intuitive decision-making*. As with athletes, analytical and rational means are used in preparation, but the final the decision is taken using intuition. Take into account a few high quality images - data fragments and subjective reasoning - often ignored by the analysts and which pertain to a more complex and realistic situation. By using the combination of these the marketer can make a final decision not solely based on the statistics or the analysis but also on the informed intuition of the marketer. He or she needs to predict the market behavior and thus to predict the fate of the market strategy in that particular market by the process of *Target-Customer Characterization*.

TARGET-CUSTOMER CHARACTERIZATION

Most marketers make one common mistake in *Target-Customer Characterization*. The mistake is that they put their focus on a target *market* or a target *segment* in aggregate instead of targeting customer individuals. Markets can never be used for this process because they are too abstract. It's not the markets that buy the products, but actual people. Since there are no existing customers from which to derive any personas the best way is to create some imaginary customers. Use these created customer images for developing a responsive approach towards their needs.

One should develop as many personas, or characterization images, as possible - each denoting one type of customer such as IT buyer, end user, administrator, corporate manager, etc... all within specific types of firms. Resist the urge to average user needs together. While one characterization may require a high value of a given attribute and another a low value, the average of the two serves no one. The next step is to reduce and prioritize this list into a few market segments that most closely suit the requirements for market targeting.

THE MARKET DEVELOPMENT Strategy Checklist

Compile the scenarios for the target niche, which means the application of the market segmentation strategy to the defined problem of crossing the chasm. This is how to solve the other problem of having low data by providing the marketer the information needed for decision making. Unfortunately, creating characterizations includes scenarios built using anecdotes and might contain misrepresentations, prejudices, etc... But it's still a tremendously valuable exercise. The scenarios describe target customers, the problems they face, how the new product answers their problems, how they will purchase the product, and what their experience would be post-purchase. The *Market Development Checklist* contains some factors used to refine the results from *Target-Customer Characterization* scenarios.

The must-have, "show-stopper" factors are:

- *Target Customer:* Is there an identifiable buyer for the product, accessible through the intended sales and marketing channels?

- *Compelling Reason to Buy:* Do conditions exist that mandate any reasonable buyer fix the problem outlined in the scenario with the new product?

- *Whole Product:* Can the company, with its partners and allies, release a whole product that answers the problem in total?

- *Competition:* Has the problem already been solved by another company, which crossed the chasm ahead of the new product?

THE nice to have factors are:

- *Partners and Allies:* Does the company have existing relationships to help create the whole product?

- *Distribution:* Is there an existing sales channel with which to get the whole product to the customer?

- *Pricing:* Does the cost of the whole product fit within the buyer's budget?

- *Positioning:* Is the company credible in this space with the target market segment?

- *Next Target Customer:* Is there potential to dominate adjacent niches?

THE PROCESSING IS DONE in two stages. In the first stage each of the imaginary scenarios is rated against the four show stopper issues. Score these on a scale of 1-5 (higher is better). Concentrate on the higher scoring scenarios. Any scenario where a show stopper score is very low tells the marketer to avoid it. A removed niche may actually be a good target once the chasm has been crossed despite being a poor target at this stage.

Next, score the remaining scenarios for the five

remaining factors and then rank according to the combined score. After this the top ranked scenarios become the top targets that can be kept under consideration. The team discusses each of the top ranked scenarios, utilizing intuitive thinking to decide upon the correct target for the initial target market segment *beachhead*.

In the discussions on the possible targets some people might make the suggestion to select two scenarios and try to cross the chasm in both of them. It's tempting, but the risk is too great. There can be ONE and ONLY ONE target market segment through which to cross the chasm in the beginning. All the efforts of the company must be directed towards that one single market segment.

Size of the target market

Bigger isn't always the better. The company might think that, since only one niche is being selected, they should select the largest one in size. Actually, it's a mistake to commit to doing so. When the company selects a really large market segment then, as a startup, they won't be able to service the entire segment. When the company is not able to service the entire segment then it risks creating a negative impact on their reputation in the market. The best thing that company can do when it comes to the size of the target market niche is to select the one that is of the same size as their existing market, or one sufficiently narrow that the company does not need to dramatically grow in order to serve it. By doing so they ensure that once they become the leader of the market they won't get swamped, but instead can then build on the success in this segment to move onto the next target segment.

4

WHOLE PRODUCT CONCEPT

Introduced by Theodore Levitt in *The Marketing Imagination* and further developed by Bill Davidow in *Marketing High Technology*, the *whole product* marketing model is extremely useful in the field of high-tech marketing. Essentially, a gap exists between the complete value proposition made to the customer - the complete solution to their problem - and what the new product can deliver on its own. To fill this gap the product needs an ecosystem of products and services around it, which come from the company, its partners, and its allies. Fully satisfying the needs of the customer in this way greatly increase the chances of success.

The four perceptions of a whole product in the market are:

- *Generic product*: The new product itself, purchased from the company.

- *Expected product*: What the customer expects to receive and what they thought they were buying.

- *Augmented product*: The product supplemented to fill in any gaps and maximize the chance of completely solving the buyer's business problem.

• *Potential product*: This represents the product's potential as more and more users come online and specific enhancements are developed to meet the customer's needs.

THE *EARLY MARKET* is satisfied with the *generic product* but when the company moves forward and tries to gain a foothold in the *mainstream markets* then it needs to deliver the *whole product* to the customer for his complete satisfaction.

THE WHOLE PRODUCT and the Technology Adoption Life Cycle

When the company is dealing with the early markets then the *generic product* will suffice the needs of its customers but when they start moving towards the right in the *Technology Adoption Life Cycle* the need for a *whole product* starts increasing and thus the company must work towards providing one so as to meet the expectation of its customers. To achieve this company includes other products of their own, forms partnerships, and relies on allies to provide others. Tactical alliances have but one purpose, which is to accelerate the assembly of the *whole product* within a specific target market segment.

HOW THE WHOLE product is linked to different sets of consumers

The customers who would least need a whole product are the *enthusiasts*. They tend to actually love the joy of assembling the bits and pieces themselves and create the version of the *whole product* exactly meeting their expectations. *Visionaries* are somewhat similar. They do not need the entire *whole product*. If they see the benefit then they won't mind creating the *whole product* themselves. In general the left side of the chasm is quite happy just with the *generic product* and wouldn't demand a *whole product*. Of course, the product doesn't stay on the left of the chasm. To *cross the chasm* the firm must satisfy the needs of the market on the right of the chasm as well. They need a complete product and services related to it. To capture the whole market provide the *whole product*.

Note too, that the sum of products and services required to deliver the *whole product* changes any time the core value proposition changes. If still entertaining the idea of going after multiple market segments, consider the different *whole product* each segment requires and how delivering on that proves impossible with current resources.

THE POSITIONING PROCESS

Positioning, in this process, is a verb. The positioning process is one of communications and it comprises of four key elements:

• *The Claim:* Reduce the value proposition to the one for which the product can claim undisputed market leadership. Does it pass the "elevator test"?

• *The Evidence:* Backup the claim with facts.

• *Communication:* Identify and address the right audience for the claim and evidence, address them in the right sequence, and with the right version.

• *Feedback and Adjustment:* React to competition's attempts to poke holes in the value proposition.

. . .

THE KEY to positioning is defining the positioning on two factors: one is the target segment which the company intends to dominate and the other is the value of the proposition the company intends to dominate. Work on the differentiation that carries the product and offers a value proposition to the customer that attracts them toward the new product.

Value proposition formula:

- For (target niche customers)
- Who are dissatisfied with (current options)
- Our product is a (new type of product)
- That provides (solution capability)
- Unlike (most likely alternative)
- We have assembled (whole product specification)

5

LAUNCH

Now comes the final point of the whole process, which involves the pricing and distribution, referred to as *Launching the Invasion* in reference to the D-Day analogy. The channel that the company decides to select should be the one with which the pragmatist buyers are most comfortable. Similarly, the pricing should make the pragmatist buyers comfortable. In selecting the distribution system choose the one that already has a relationship with the target customers or is in a position to create one. Understand how to fit the selected channel into the product mix.

The major distribution channels that exist in high tech marketing are:

- *Direct Sales:* The dedicated sales force employed by the company.

- *Two-Tier Retail:* In this distribution strategy the distributor acts as the first tier and the retailer as the second tier for distribution. The vendor ships to the distributor and then the distributor manages inventory and the retailers.

- *One-Tier Retail:* In this type of channel, one single store acts as both the wholesaler and the retailer.

- *Internet Retail:* This can be both single tier and two-tier and is generally used for products that don't require much support from the vendor.

- *Two-Tier Value Added Reseller:* VAR sales are for products that require some additional supports as well such as installation, configuration, etc.

- *OEMs:* Selling the products to manufacturers who use the product integrated into their own system.

- *System integrators:* This is a system which is project oriented and is generally for managing very large or very complex computer projects.

THE DIRECT SALES method of distribution is generally the best method for *crossing the chasm*. Getting a firm's direct sales force into the *pragmatist*'s domain may require the help of a partner which already has a relationship with the targeted customers and who is ready to use that relationship for the new product's benefit.

PRICING

The pricing of the products is a major decision and also one of the toughest as it involves a number of different perspectives. *Customer-Oriented pricing* leads to the highest chance of success. This concentrates on the customer's perspective and what value is delivered. *Value based pricing* matches the value of the result to the price charged. It's suited to the *visionaries* as they are often ready to pay high prices in return of their expectation of a really high return. The conservatives, meanwhile, would want a low price. It's their reward for buying late, when competition means cost dictates prices - known as *cost based pricing*.

The *pragmatists* lie between these two. Since *crossing the chasm* depends upon this group, they become the main concern. Unlike the previous groups, the whole product cost concerns them very much. This includes the buying cost as well as the cost of ownership. They expect some competitive advantage from their investment in the product and they're willing to pay a little premium when purchasing from the market leader, depending on the market prices prevailing at that time. This type of pricing is called the *competition based pricing*.

The final pricing model is *distribution-oriented pricing*. There can be two factors that influence the distribution channel motivation: is the product priced to sell and is it actually worthwhile to sell the product? This means that the price isn't so high that it becomes an obstacle in selling the product. It's often seen that when companies are trying to cross the chasm they tend to price the product high for higher margins. But at some point of time it actually becomes an issue for the pragmatist buyers and defeats the whole purpose.

TECHNOLOGY ADOPTION LIFE CYCLE

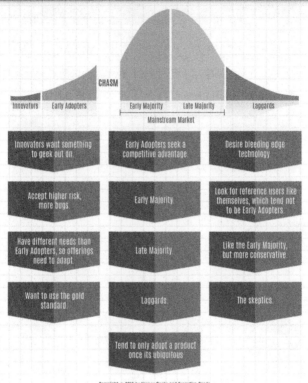

CHASM

Innovators | Early Adopters | Early Majority | Late Majority | Laggards

Mainstream Market

Innovators want something to geek out on.	Early Adopters seek a competitive advantage.	Desire bleeding edge technology
Accept higher risk, more bugs.	Early Majority.	Look for reference users like themselves, which tend not to be Early Adopters.
Have different needs than Early Adopters, so offerings need to adapt	Late Majority.	Like the Early Majority, but more conservative.
Want to use the gold standard.	Laggards.	The skeptics.
	Tend to only adopt a product once its ubiquitous	

Book Summary of Crossing the Chasm by Geoffrey Moore

BASIC PLAN:

1 Build momentum and use it to swing from vine to vine as success with one group leads to success with the next.

2 Build beachheads in target segments within the Early Majority in order to cross the Chasm.

3 Focus on niche segments from which a wider base can be built.

4 Update the product offering to appeal to the needs of the Early Majority, which likely won't match up with what made the product successful with Innovators and Early Adopters.

5 Continuous Innovation: Improvements to a product which don't drastically change how its used.

6 Discontinuous Innovation: Improvements which require a user to change their patterns or equipment in order to use. This is not necessarily Disruptive Innovation.

FACTORS:

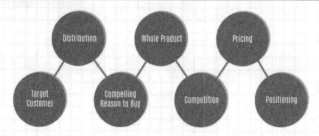

Distribution · Whole Product · Pricing · Target Customer · Compelling Reason to Buy · Competition · Positioning

Book Summary of Crossing the Chasm by Geoffrey Moore   Executive Reads

THE WHOLE PRODUCT MODEL

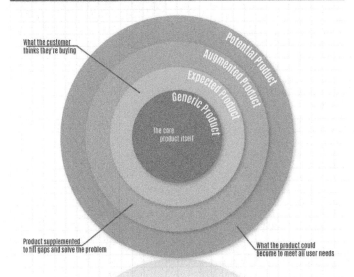

What the customer thinks they're buying

Potential Product

Augmented Product

Expected Product

Generic Product

the core product itself

Product supplemented to fill gaps and solve the problem

What the product could become to meet all user needs

Thank you for reading the Executive Reads summary of Geoffrey A. Moore's, *Crossing the Chasm*.

If you enjoyed this summary, please follow this link to take a moment to leave a review, which helps others find it.

For your convenience we provide a downloadable PDF of the infographic.

http://ereads.xyz/2334C

Infographic

To keep up-to-date with Executive Reads news, releases, freebies, or business article summaries (you choose), subscribe to our newsletter. We never share your information with anybody.

If you have feedback, good or bad, we'd love to hear from you at: feedback@executivereads.com.

ALSO FROM EXECUTIVE READS

Crucial Conversations

http://ereads.xyz/CrucialConvos

Available in ebook, paperback, and audiobook.

Crucial Conversations: Tools for Talking When Stakes Are High guides you in conducting conversations when they matter most. Handle these delicate situations with attention, purpose, and calm.

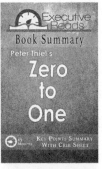

Zero to One

http://ereads.xyz/ZeroToOne

Available in ebook, and paperback.

Zero to One: Notes on Startups, or How to Build the Future details Peter Thiel's ideas on creating not just a new company, but a monopoly for an idea.

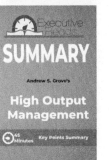

High Output Management

http://ereads.xyz/HighOutput

Available in ebook and paperback and audiobook.

High Output Management takes the reader through the fundamentals of organizational leverage. It lays out the principles underlying Grove's success at Intel and the result driven methodology.